Me and My Friends

I Can Share

written by Daniel Nunn

illustrated by Clare Elsom

raintree
a Capstone company — publishers for children

Raintree is an imprint of Capstone Global Library Limited, a company incorporated in England and Wales having its registered office at 7 Pilgrim Street, London, EC4V 6LB – Registered company number: 6695582

www.raintreepublishers.co.uk
myorders@raintreepublishers.co.uk

Text © Capstone Global Library Limited 2015
First published in paperback in 2015
The moral rights of the proprietor have been asserted.

Edited by Brynn Baker
Designed by Steve Mead and Kyle Grenz
Production by Helen McCreath
Original illustrations © Clare Elsom
Originated by Capstone Global Library Ltd
Printed and bound in China by LEO

ISBN 978 1 406 28163 7 (hardback)
18 17 16 15 14
10 9 8 7 6 5 4 3 2 1

ISBN 978-1-406-28168-2 (paperback)
19 18 17 16 15
10 9 8 7 6 5 4 3 2 1

British Library Cataloguing in Publication Data
A full catalogue record for this book is available from the British Library.

Contents

Sharing

I share with my friend.

My friends share with me.

I share my games.

My friend shares with me.

I share my apple.

My friend shares with me.

I share my crayons.

My friends share with me.

I share my spade.

My friend shares with me.

I share my books.

My friend shares with me.

I share my bike.

My friend shares with me.

I share with my friends.

We have fun when we share!

Sharing quiz

Which of these pictures
shows sharing?

Did sharing make these children happy? Why? Do you like to share?

Picture glossary

friend person you care about and have fun with

share to divide up between you and your friends, or take turns using something

Index

Notes for teachers and parents

BEFORE READING

Building background: Ask children what it means to share. Ask them to name some things they share with family members, classmates and friends. Is it hard to share? Why or why not?

AFTER READING

Recall and reflection: Ask the class how children in the book had fun. (Playing games, reading books.) What do we need to do to be a good friend? (Take turns, share.)

Sentence knowledge: Ask children to find a capital letter and a full stop in the book. Ask what a capital letter and a full stop signify.

Word knowledge (phonics): Ask children to point to the word *share* on page 4. Sound out the three phonemes in the word *sh/a/re*. Ask children to sound out each phoneme as they point to the letters, and then blend the sounds together to make the word *share*. Can they think of other words that start with the sound *sh*? (Shadow, shake, shout.)

Word recognition: Ask children to count how many times *share/shares* appears in the main text (not counting the quiz). (16)

AFTER-READING ACTIVITIES

Place children in small groups to write and draw about something they share with friends. Give each child only one tool, such as crayons, scissors, pencils and so on. Children will need to share the materials to complete the work.

In this book

Topic
sharing

Topic words
apple
bike
books
crayons
friend
games
share
spade

High-frequency words
have
I
me
my
we
when
with

Sentence stems
I ____ with my ___.
My ___ shares with ___.
I ___ my ___.
We have ___ when we ___.